BÔ YIN RÂ
(J. A. SCHNEIDERFRANKEN)

THE GATED GARDEN
VOLUME NINE

THE BOOK OF DIALOGUES

For more information
about the books of Bô Yin Râ and
titles published in English translation,
visit The Kober Press web site at
www.kober.com.

BÔ YIN RÂ
(J. A. SCHNEIDERFRANKEN)

THE BOOK OF DIALOGUES

TRANSLATED FROM THE GERMAN
BY B.A. REICHENBACH

BERKELEY, CALIFORNIA

Copyright © 2007 by B. A. Reichenbach
Eric W. Strauss, Publisher & Editor
All rights reserved.

For permission to quote or excerpt, write to:
THE KOBER PRESS
2534 Chilton Way
Berkeley, California 94704
email: koberpress@mindspring.com

This book is a translation from the German of *Das Buch der Gespräche* by Bô Yin Râ (J.A. Schneiderfranken), published in 1920 by Verlag der Weißen Bücher (Kurt Wolff), München. The copyright to the German text is held by Kober Verlag, AG, Bern, Switzerland.

Printed in the United States of America

International Standard Book Number: 978-0-915034-14-X

Typography and composition by Dickie Magidoff, Burney, CA

Book cover after a design by Bô Yin Râ

ACKNOWLEDGMENT

For her careful reading and
many thoughtful suggestions
I again owe thanks to
Alice Glawe

CONTENTS

Testimony 9
1 Knowledge and Reality in Action 13
2 Light and Darkness 25
3 The Spirit's Might 31
4 The Jewel of the Heart 37
5 Transformation 41
6 The Dialogue on the
   Innermost East 47
7 The Dialogue on the
   Parting of a Master 53
8 The Flower Garden 59
9 The Deviant Pupils 67

10	Night of Trial	75
11	Individuality and Person	83
12	The Realm of the Soul	89
13	On Finding Oneself	107
14	On the Elder Brothers of Mankind	115
15	Mysteries of Magic	131

TESTIMONY

Stars everlasting I witnessed ablaze
That no one saw ever appear;
Things closest dissolved into vanishing haze,
Things farthest away I found near.

Sounds I felt stirring chords in my soul
That seldom another had heard;
Words that I met, within me would toll
To reveal the primordial word.

All who before me masters had been
As brothers now gave me their hand.
Recovered from dreams at last I have seen
And entered the luminous land.

There I received my own consecration
From the sons of all-governing might;
After long years of hard preparation
They guided their brother toward light.

Imbued with light's ocean I henceforth am one,
Like a drop in an infinite sea.
What now lies behind me forever is gone
And of its mirage I am free.

Thus have I found what very few find;
I beheld what most seek in vain;
In mortal existence closely confined
I recovered my soul's timeless reign.

Yet if from this earth one ever should see
My heartfelt affection withheld,
Then also my spirit would have to flee,
From radiant dimensions expelled.

CHAPTER ONE

KNOWLEDGE AND REALITY IN ACTION

Wʜᴇɴ ᴀғᴛᴇʀ ᴍᴀɴʏ ʏᴇᴀʀs I once more had the privilege of holding the hand of the venerated teacher to whom I owe all things I have received; when first I saw his radiant eyes shine with compassion in the sunlight of the South and heard his quiet voice, I told him of the joy I felt that now I would be given, also personally from his lips, that last and final knowledge whose mysteries so very few are able to experience on this earth. And at that time I still believed this knowledge to comprise essentially the teachings of a secret kind of "science," comparable to the disciplines pursued on earth, but not to be transmitted except to tried and tested pupils.

The venerable Master smiled as he looked at me and for a long time remained silent.

Finally he said, "You are a typical son of the West. Whatever is not shown you in the form of 'science,' you look upon as doubtful; and so you dare not trust the truth unless it stands before you in the guise of 'science,' as that word is understood by schools of higher learning in your country.

"You will have to learn a different way of knowing truth, my friend!

"You need to learn to comprehend a manner of instruction that differs from the kind that is exclusively pursued and recognized throughout your world.

"If you mean to find the truth you first and foremost need to rid yourself of the illusion that truth consists of 'knowledge' one can 'learn.'

"Your search must henceforth be directed toward a different goal.

"Your quest must be to probe reality in action."

And after having paused again a while, he continued,

"The world of the soul is life unceasingly in action.

"The world of the soul cannot reveal its mysteries to you unless you enter that dynamic realm, which lies beyond the grasp of mortal senses, and thus become a witness of its works.

"Then only will you find the very wisdom that even the wisest of the wise can never 'know'; for it is truly known by only those who have *experienced* this reality within themselves and who are capable of doing this at will, at any time."

When the venerable teacher had ended his remarks there followed a long silence; only the scornful call of a pepper bird interrupted the quiet now and then. The Master's eyes looked far away, across the silver-grayish clouds of foliage spreading in the olive groves, while in my mind I formed the question whether even for that other form of knowing a certain level of culture and of learning might not be a necessary precondition.

At that point the radiant sage, having observed my question taking form within my mind—because he understood my native language only with some difficulty and so had to communicate with me by spiritual means, even in close physical proximity—began to speak again and said,

"Worldly culture, education, depth of learning, aesthetic refinement, appreciation of the arts, and philosophy—in short, all the accomplishments your thoughts surveyed when forming your question are utterly irrelevant factors in the quest for final truth.

"What your schools define as 'speculative philosophy'—a discipline that has been practiced for millennia also in my native land, which well may be the cradle of that practice of pursuing 'science,'—is in effect a paralyzing influence upon the spiritual energies that make it possible for human beings to experience spiritual reality.

"In this respect our men of learning are in error when they think that by this method they have found the final source of truth; and here your scholars in the West are equally in error when full of awe they marvel at the depth of our thought, assuming its results present the ultimate perception one is able to attain of truth.

"Again, it is no accident that also in the West there have been men of razor-sharp intelligence who, by virtue of their thinking, arrived at similar, if not indeed identical, results as did the thinkers found in our lands.

"Even as when playing chess the possible configurations of the pieces are past counting, and yet the game is always played exclusively within the limits of the board, so, too, are all the insights one may gain through thinking forever subject to the laws that govern thought and cannot ever leave the confines of the field on which they play.

"The object, however, that one wishes to attain by way of thought lies far beyond the chess board of the mind; and even though it may become the subject matter of one's thought—*after* it has been attained—at no time is it ever found by thinking."

AND AFTER ANOTHER brief pause, during which the Master explained to my companion— a woman from a family of scholars, well informed in every field of learning—the differences between Eastern and Western traditions of teaching, he continued, saying,

"In order to discover 'the philosophers' stone' —the final truth—the innermost secret of secrets, the wellspring of the Origin, the ultimate source of peace, the goal that stills all yearning: to accomplish that one does not need to know that the earth orbits the sun; that the stars at night are not lanterns set in the dome of the sky but cosmic bodies; nor what the causes are that set off lightning and thunder, and more things of that nature, which the human mind was able to unravel.

"All such knowledge is at last completely useless in the quest for the Ground of Being.

"The sun could move around the earth each day; thunder and lightning could be demonstrations of demonic powers; and the stars could well be lampions lit above our heads each night by spirits of the air.

"All these things are to be judged as wholly unessential in the search for final truth, for the experience of eternal life.

KNOWLEDGE AND REALITY IN ACTION

"Any random fiction to explain all these phenomena would serve the human being just as well as the most solidly established knowledge, proven by experiments with complicated instruments, designed to illustrate the working laws of nature.

"We regret that humans came to place such disproportionate value on such knowledge, because it makes the mortal's quest to find the Spirit's life increasingly more difficult.

"As a result of all this knowledge humans lose a world of feelings in which they should remain at home.

"Mortals build themselves through instruments gigantic organs of perception, which expand their mental universe, but are no longer matched at all by their innate capacities to comprehend; and they deceive themselves assuming that by virtue of this mass of mental knowledge, which far exceeds their actual effective powers, they have come closer to the final truth they ultimately seek by so much as the width of a hair.

'The only thing that humans thus accomplish is the painful recognition of their given lack of power, a feeling of disharmony between the things they 'know' and what they can 'achieve.'

"This sense of being powerless will then mislead them to dismiss the real power they possess, albeit through their spiritual nature, while at the same time they point proudly at their great 'inventions,' unaware it is precisely these that rob them of their greatest gift, because they keep the human will pursuing a direction exactly opposite to where the goal it truly seeks can be attained.

"Humans thus lose the capacity to sense that all phenomena within the outer world are ultimately relative; they can no longer fathom that the 'laws of nature' they believe to have discovered—even if they did so quite correctly—are themselves conditionally dependent; and that the power of the Spirit, while it cannot change the 'laws' of the external world, nonetheless is able to alter the conditions that affect these laws.

"The realm of the *eternal*, on the other hand, which mortal man with all his efforts finally desires to uncover, with increasing clarity, will permanently lie beyond his grasp—unless he changes the direction of his search.

"Tomorrow already this entire cosmos of immeasurable space could find itself reduced to dust; another universe with wholly different conditions could occupy this boundless space; 'laws of nature' could become effective of which your 'science' still has no idea; yet in the Spirit's realm, which can be apprehended only through experience, not one iota would have changed.

"VAIN AND FLEETING is the haughty 'knowledge' that modern minds endeavor to attain in the external realm; vain and fleeting are the fancied 'insights' that depend upon the crutches of philosophy and speculation; but the apprehension of the inmost essence of reality, acquired by experience, will make the most unlearned beggar, who never heard of what your world regards as 'culture' and 'progress,' only sits in his hut in the forest and lives on the offerings of pilgrims who have to cross the jungle—an eternal king of all the worlds, a master of all life.

"To be sure, you ought not to retire to the jungle, imitating such a yogi; indeed, it is desirable that one who is a pupil striving after wisdom as a member of the Western world will have at his disposal enough of the external knowledge of his time that he can reach the people of his country in the language of his age; but all such outer learning must not obstruct the path that leads him, by virtue of experience, to knowledge of the Spirit; nor must it turn into a fetter that impedes his stride.

"Not until he has transcended his external 'knowledge' may he earnestly expect to find the certainty of final *knowledge*, by virtue of *experiencing* the Spirit in himself."

CHAPTER TWO

LIGHT AND DARKNESS

At that time I one day asked the venerable master whether it was true, as I had heard, that there were human beings living on this earth who had been granted knowledge of life's final secrets and possessed great spiritual power, which they used, however, only to the end of doing mankind harm.

And the venerated teacher said,

"Whoever is admitted to the sublime community of Luminaries is henceforth obligated by eternal law to shine, both for himself and others, as a sun of cosmic space.

"If he continued then to borrow his light from others, as it still might be permitted to a pupil, he would inexorably forfeit the divine creative powers entrusted to his will.

"For him, who has become an 'eye that sees the worlds,' there must no longer be confusion of whatever kind, because in him abides a power holding him accountable for every moment lived throughout his life.

"With kings and beggars must he learn to speak as if he were himself a member of their class; and he must only see the *human* essence in each mortal, must learn to disregard the accidents of rank and status, guilt and merit, crown and humble beggar's staff.

"No mortal human power shall deceive, nor hold him in its spell; for any show of might he may encounter has in itself its limits and its end; the power, on the other hand, which consciously his will embodies, and which he serves, even though he has authority to use it and must direct it by his will, is infinite within itself.

"However closely he might feel himself attached to mortal human life, he even so is at the same time free of it at every moment, because his soul became a 'kingdom of eternity.'

"No force outside himself can ever strip him of that kingdom's crown and scepter.

"He alone is able to destroy himself through guilt by his own fault.

"Yet while he thus might 'fall,' he nonetheless remains connected to the power whose vessel he was made, even after having 'fallen.'

"He then will count among the forces of destruction, which are as necessary in the sea of physical existence as turbulence and storms are needed by the oceans of the earth.

"Those who once had known him as a friend and Brother, now meet him as an enemy; and the sublime community must grieve for the loss of a star who caused himself to fall, by his own will, into the abysmal chaos of eternal dissolution.

"Surrounded by profoundest darkness, without the strength to rise again, he now lives solely for the will that works destruction, until at last he is consumed by his own will and thus disintegrates into uncounted particles of energy, which then begin the pilgrimage of life anew, as liberated elements of power.

"THE SAME ETERNAL energy is manifest in both the 'Luminary' as in his fallen counterpart, 'the lord of darkness'; and this sovereign of the abyss, embodying the impulse of destruction, would not possess his might had he not once received it as a 'Luminary.'

"By his fall from radiant Light he joined the 'Brothers of Darkness.'

"That is the truth behind the things you heard; and also in the Western world there are innumerable individuals who live completely unaware of being merely puppets dominated by these powerful destroyers, wholly subject to their mighty will."

CHAPTER THREE

THE SPIRIT'S MIGHT

Again I one day asked the venerable sage who at that time conveyed to me his knowledge, before I, too, was able to *become* objective "knowledge in the Spirit," whether one might not perhaps, despite his reservations, find in ancient books, kept secret by "initiates," both traces of authentic wisdom and methods to acquire hidden skills—and he replied,

"With greater joy should you receive the smallest insight that your spirit grants you than welcome all the weight of knowledge gained through study.

"More should you delight in the smallest success your spirit may let you achieve than in all the craftsmanship and knowledge one can learn on earth.

"You want to stay away from those who must have 'learned' all things they seek to know and do.

"You want to stay away from those who must have 'heard' or 'read' whatever 'knowledge' they possess.

"Your spirit needs to be at all times free, so that it may in freedom exercise its powers.

"Your spirit is to be continuously lord and master of all the energies your soul contains, so that it may unite them under its control.

"Your soul, in truth, embodies energies whose depth no one has ever fully probed; and also in your body there are many hidden powers no one has as yet completely fathomed in himself.

"I want to lift your body's bonds to set it free and give it life; and I shall make the forces of your soul your faithful servants, eager at all time to serve your will.

"You should not have to glean from books the wisdom you attain, nor borrow from another the force that lets you act.

"You have within yourself the most experienced, skillful teacher and all the wisdom written down in books is insignificant beside the treasures gathered in your soul."

CHAPTER FOUR

THE JEWEL OF THE HEART

ON ANOTHER OCCASION THE question discussed was how the experience of this earthly life was to be valued in the Spirit's light, and the exalted sage gave this advice:

"You are to grind and polish your experience like a diamond—using its own dust.

"You are to 'set' your temporal experience as if it were a precious gem.

"All your experience must be polishable into clear-cut facets, letting them reflect the heaven's light, even as in forms of geometric order.

"Like a goldsmith must you seek with patience to create the 'golden ring' that is allowed to serve your 'finely cut' experience as its worthy 'setting.'

"You are the author of your own experience.

"You likewise are yourself its 'setting.'

"You are yourself the gemstone's cutter and the goldsmith of the ring that is your life.

"The jewel you shall thus create—present it as a gift to the Eternal.

"Offer your own self to the Eternal as a precious gem.

"Within His treasury you shall be well protected and secure.

"As a jewel of the heart shall your experience gleam forever in the radiance of eternity."

CHAPTER FIVE

TRANSFORMATION

Bᴜᴛ ᴏɴ ᴀ ᴅɪꜰꜰᴇʀᴇɴᴛ ᴏᴄᴄᴀꜱɪᴏɴ during the time when I was still my venerated guru's chela, he one day taught me, saying,

"Behold the beast with its multitude of heads!

"You have set out to slay the beast, but every head you severed has grown back again each time anew and threatens you the same way as before.

"Whoever would destroy that beast must do so without shedding its blood.

"See that you destroy the beast by appearing to follow its will!

"Treat the beast with kindness—for in that way it finally shall perish."

And I followed the instruction I was given, even though in those days the advice to me made little sense.

I had to be "kind" to the beast for a long time before at last it seemed to recognize that there was someone whom its presence could not frighten.

Time and again it tried to invade me with dread; and, truly, it knew to be dreadful.

But in the end the day arrived when for the last time I had to treat it with "kindness"—more, indeed, than ever before—and tired the beast lay down and perished.

The waves of an ocean older than the world carried its body away.

From that day on my soul could feel it had gained freedom from all servitude.

I now was able, at will, either to float above my mortal body, or to seek shelter in it, like a snail within its shell.

Now I had become the master where before I only was a slave.

And the voice of the Law came to me and said,

"Because you have loosed what had been bound in your kind from the beginning of the earth, you henceforth shall have power to bind and to loose what is of your kind."

Thus was I granted power in those days to dominate a host of unseen forces.

From that time on, however, my Brothers in the Spirit said,

"The Western world is given a new teacher. The stars of the Occident have not yet ceased to shine."

As of that day it was to be my solemn obligation in dialogues and images to teach as much as may be taught that way. Thus I began to form in my own words what now the Spirit of Eternity permitted me to apprehend, directly without words, as well as personal insights granted me on my own path into the Spirit, to the extent I was allowed to make them public.

I now was obligated to guide others to themselves, given that I had myself become the "knowledge born of certainty."

I offer what I have to give and in the way that I am able to present it.

In all my writings there is not a single word that would not be considered with attention.

At times a question may arise in a particular passage, but find its answer only in a different context. One needs to bear in mind, however, that answers one may offer here are strictly limited and that these limits are not ever to be crossed.

CHAPTER SIX

THE DIALOGUE ON THE INNERMOST EAST

HIS PUPILS ONE DAY ASKED a sage about the "wise men of the East," and he answered them, saying,

"Seek the 'innermost East' within you!

"Once you live in the 'innermost East' yourselves, you shall encounter the 'wise men of the East,'—but not before that day.

"Whoever discovers the 'East' within himself will have attained a 'realm' far greater than all kingdoms of the earth.

"THE MERCIFUL, THE All-Compassionate—blessed be His name—is like unto a Shah-in-Shah whose rule embraces every kingdom of the world.

"With justice and compassion he chooses kings to rule the countries of the Spirit's world, endowing them with might and wisdom to be stewards, guarding their entrusted reigns, but He alone remains the sovereign of all lands.

"Within the inmost center of the heart, within yourselves, there is an anteroom, no larger than a mustard seed; and therein is a tiny portal, smaller than a speckle in a sunbeam.

"Through this portal must he squeeze himself who seeks to enter the 'innermost East.'

"Having crossed that portal, he shall find beyond it lands expanding without end—an everlasting 'earth'—an 'India' embodying all Indias—a 'mountain range' that dwarfs all other mountains.

"There shall he find the realm that is his own, forever founded from eternity.

"Before he can approach the kingdom, however, which in these lands will be bestowed upon him by that Shah-in-Shah, who there holds sway through all eternity, he first must reach the sacred river that continuously circles the inner regions of that country; a river having neither source nor mouth, which constantly begets and swallows up itself.

"Here he shall encounter the river's 'ferryman'; and the ferryman will ask him for his 'name'.

"If then he does not know his 'name', he must without exception return again at once to the external earth.

"But if he is able to answer the ferryman's question, he will take him to the river's other bank, where he shall find himself in the 'innermost East.'

"Here he shall meet the guide who will lead him to the 'towering mountains' in the 'innermost East.'

"There, amidst forever snow-capped peaks he unexpectedly will come upon green meadows covered with blooming flowers, so that his wonderment will have no bounds.

"There he shall behold the domes of a majestic temple soaring to the skies; and when at last he reaches it and is allowed to enter, he finally will in that temple also find the 'wise men of the East,' for whom he until then had always searched in vain."

But when his pupils further sought to know whether it was absolutely necessary that a soul should find the 'wise men of the East' if it desired one day to attain its spiritual kingdom, the sage replied,

"You do not know what you are asking!

"Whoever sets out to attain the kingdom of his soul requires guidance from within if his pursuit is to succeed.

"That inner help, however, can only be provided by the few that live within the 'inmost East'; the few the All-Compassionate endowed with power to bring light to those among their 'brothers in the darkness' whose earnest *will*, not merely *wishful thinking*, truly wants to find such light.

"Consequently, you will have to find the 'wise men of the East' within you if ever you expect to gain the inner kingdom that is yours."

CHAPTER SEVEN

THE DIALOGUE ON THE PARTING OF A MASTER

"**A**ND WHAT OCCURS," A PUPIL asked his teacher, "whenever one of that sublime community departs this mortal life? Will he then disappear within the boundless ocean of the Spirit's light, aware of only his own self within that radiant sea—will he still live in spiritual unity with his exalted Brothers, united with them purely through his spirit—or will he even then continue in some way to be connected with the earth?"

And the Master responded, saying,

"When the Anointed feels the end of the days approaching that bound him to the garment of the earth, he then delivers both himself and the eternal power to which he owed the radiance shared in Oneness to another member in the cosmic chain, whose timeless human self the sun had likewise set aflame, in order that he one day might become the Anointed one's successor in the lives of human beings of his day.

"Until that time the latter still was the anointed teacher's pupil, even though he, too, had long since been a Master among the Masters of the Seven Gates.

"Now the one departing will say to his successor,

'Today you shall through me become the Way; for I myself have been the Way, which I have now transcended.

'Two are henceforth One, and from the Two shall rise the Third—this truth conceals the secret of your being unified with me.

'The head of Janus keeps forever turning.

'The old gives way to the young and the young in turn becomes the old.

'But from themselves the Two beget the Third—the One who stays eternally in Being and must abide wherever life exists.

THE DIALOGUE ON THE PARTING OF A MASTER

'The power flowing through the core of the chain gives life to both the old and to the young, and likewise to the One whom both are forming of themselves.

'Thus, interwoven in the chain throughout all coming ages, I now bid you to manifest the light pervading both of us.

'I now lay down the mortal garment of the earth.

'What it had veiled, I give into your hands.

'I now conceal myself within you; for I belong to those who will abide with humankind on earth as helpers, and in the same way also you belong to us.

'We cannot ever leave this earth, not in this nor any future aeon, before the last of human spirits has regained the realm of light.

'No mystery is found on earth to equal this.'

"Thus will the Anointed unify his spirit with him who until then had been his pupil and from that day on both shall be as one."

CHAPTER EIGHT

THE FLOWER GARDEN

"Here, where flowers now are growing in abundance, only a few years ago you would have seen no more than a deserted wilderness.

"Weeds luxuriated in profusion where roses bloom today; and every kind of vermin had made these grounds its paradise.

"Narcissus blossoms now exude their fragrance from the very soil that not so long ago had brought forth only putrid vegetation.

"And both alike the same sun quickens from the selfsame earth."

Those were the words of the gardener.

But I will show to you a garden of a different kind; one in which you shall yourself become the gardener.

The things said of that other garden, you cannot claim yet of your own.

From dawn to dusk you pluck out weeds and then expect that flowers ought to grow; but all you ever get is still another crop of weeds.

And now you quarrel with a "God," who is your own invention, and want him to reward you with the fruits your labors earned, instead of sowing on your own and to request for that the necessary seed from those whose flower beds already stand in bloom.

The "God" you call upon is but the shadow of your anguish-ridden heart.

From him do not expect returns for all your pains!

Your *living god*—the true and only God your soul desires—will not appear inside your "garden" until the seed you had requested from the elder gardeners' flowering grounds shall have begun to sprout.

THE FLOWER GARDEN

You may consider all of human life as such to be "deserted wilderness," yet it is land that only waits for gardeners who will transform it into "flowering gardens."

The very "earth" and "sun" shall then make only "flowers" grow where nothing more than "weeds" abound today.

The goals that you have set yourself are high.

You strive for everything that can inspire your ascent.

Only one thing you have always overlooked:

Namely, that you cannot hope for bloom to grow where you have not yourself sowed any seed.

That "seed," however, you first have to request from others: from gardeners whose flowers have already blossomed.

Be assured, they willingly shall give you of their flowers' seed. Only you cannot believe that from these inconspicuous grains there one day could grow blossoms.

And so you heedlessly discard the seed that you were given; and others, who may later come along that way, will then discover wondrous, brilliant flowers by the roadside, while you grow only weeds in your own garden as before.

Or, if indeed you put the seed into the ground, you then each day dig up the soil again to quell the doubt that makes you question whether the requested flower seed that you were given truly had the strength to sprout.

But in that way you never shall see flowers!

All things that grow want quiet and profound seclusion.

If then at last you want your garden full of flowers, you truly have to do what must be done.

Go to the elder gardeners whose flower seed is ready; ask them for some and carefully collect what you receive.

Then spread that seed on soil that you have well prepared and leave it to the earth and to the sun to make it sprout and grow to bring you flowers.

THE FLOWER GARDEN

Be not concerned if here and there some weeds still should appear among the growing blossoms.

Once your flowers truly have begun to bloom, you will find it easy to get rid of weeds.

Your everlasting, living God shall only come into your garden when all its flower beds are found in bloom.

You must not try to force their growth by artificial means!

You need to do no more than till the ground and sow the seed.

For all things else you have to trust the earth and the sun.

On your earth, too, the sun shall spread its rays.

If, my friend, you thoroughly have tilled the soil and sowed the seed with care, your living God shall finally be born to you on your own garden's earth.

Its blooming flowers' fragrance will then become his nourishment.

In sacred silence shall his wondrous form unfold itself.

Along the paths of your own garden, when all its flowers stand in bloom, you one day shall be walking with your God.

CHAPTER NINE

THE DEVIANT PUPILS

A CERTAIN MASTER LIVED IN A great city where ships from many countries found their harbor, so that it was not long before he saw himself surrounded by numerous pupils.

There were some who carefully collected his words.

As years went by they "knew" nearly all of his sayings and almost had forgotten that his words were not their own.

They were revered as sages, both in the city and in distant lands, and people turned to them when they felt need to know the Master's thoughts.

Others of his pupils would listen to the sound of his words with open hearts, but the form of his speech did not linger in their memory.

The Master's teachings, however, lent structure to their lives and no event occurred in their surroundings they did not see but through the Master's eyes.

Again there were some who felt enraptured by the Master's words and let them sink into the depth of their souls; and thus they also lived according to his teachings, but following, instead, their own souls' inspiration. In doing this they learned to see with their own eyes, not in the way the Master saw, but as he wanted things to be perceived.

After some time, however, there rose within their souls a way of knowing that was new and thoroughly their own.

Their souls' own way of knowing struggled with the Master's teachings and, growing ever stronger in that contest, triumphed in the end.

But now their own new understanding made them grasp the Master's words in ways they never had been understood before.

P<small>EOPLE IN THE MASTER'S</small> city therefore said, "Shame upon these deviant pupils! They cannot comprehend the venerable sage's teachings and so his wisdom has deserted them.

"How very sad he was to find such listeners who could not hear, such worshipers without devotion!"

O<small>NE DAY STRANGERS CAME</small> into the Master's city; men from distant shores who sought to find surviving traces of his wisdom; for the sage himself had long since passed away.

In their search they went from place to place but no one could present them with the wisdom they had hoped to find.

At last they also came to those who in the Master's city were rejected as the "deviant pupils" and very soon their hearts were set on fire because they recognized that only here the Master's wisdom had been fully comprehended; but also that his teachings had brought forth a greater doctrine, one that in itself contained all things the Master's own words had not touched upon.

Their souls profoundly joyful and enriched, they now returned again to the distant shores of their native land and everywhere throughout their country made the newer doctrine known, wherein the Master's teachings had been given a new form.

Not until a long time later did the people in the Master's city learn that far beyond the seas the teachings of the "deviant pupils" had already gained acceptance as the wisdom that alone embraced the Master's deepest insights.

Greatly astonished they assembled to take counsel and, having decided, said,

"Let us from that distant country bring a teacher we can trust; for who can tell what passes for the doctrine of these 'deviant pupils' in those parts?"

And so they sent a ship that was to bring them such a teacher from that land.

THE DEVIANT PUPILS

Yet when their envoys arrived, they found no teacher of the newer wisdom who was willing to return with then. Instead, they all insisted, saying, "But in your midst you have your own enlightened teachers! And they alone had made us find the wisdom that we teach. How could we ever hope to bring you from afar what we in fact were given by your city? How could we even dare to teach among you, being only pupils of your masters, who had perfected their great Master's teachings?"

But as the envoys did not want to sail back empty-handed, they kept on searching till at last they found a man who was prepared to go with them because they promised him a large reward.

However, he was someone who had not fully understood the newer teachings and thus found no respect among authentic teachers.

Now, when he came into the Master's city and began to teach, everyone listened to him with attention and all were pleased to have so "great" a teacher in their midst; the more so as the things he taught turned out to be quite different from the teachings of the "deviant pupils."

And so the people said, "How very foolish, truly, were those messengers who once had come here from afar to learn the venerated Master's wisdom from these 'deviant pupils'!

"Only now do we completely understand the Master!

"None but this 'great teacher' from afar has made us fully understand his wisdom!

"He alone, indeed, is worthy to be honored as the great successor of the venerated Master who once had lived in our midst."

And that remained their firm, unshakable conviction.

CHAPTER TEN

NIGHT OF TRIAL

It was in the days when I was still my venerable guru's pupil.

It was in the days when I had yet to prove that I was able to become my Master's "Brother."

Silently, from deepest grounds of darkness, night appeared to rise like water welling from a spring.

The valleys moved closer together and the mountains raised themselves as if for battle.

Heavy-winged, from dizzying heights an eagle plunged with deafening roar.

Then, only silence surrounded me, making the blood in my veins rush with the sound of a river.

My spirit was drowning in sadness and even torrents of melancholy could not have deepened its anguish,

Motionless, resembling the shrouded host on Good Friday, the moon emerged, a sight of rigid life, from clouds as if in pains of labor.

Trembling in every fiber, my body felt its imminent destruction, weakened by the tests it had endured before.

Invisibly, some monstrous force now seemed resolved to strangle it.

THEN, SUDDENLY, MY EYES were opened and could see—in a new and different way—and what they saw were creatures of decaying worlds; creatures that did not appear to suffer being heinous; for I could feel they found themselves supremely beautiful in their abominable loathsomeness.

Paralyzing horror issued from their sight and when my eyes were forced to meet their slimy glances, a thousand poisoned arrows struck my heart.

They, however, reveled in their heinousness and each new wound from which my arrow-riddled heart began to bleed increased their gruesome lust.

I wanted the earth to swallow me in my torment and would rather have offered my flesh to the wolves than fall prey to these odious fiends; but the earth would not open to save me and even the wolves fled the site of such horrors.

My soul cried out in unbearable pain and my body writhed like a trodden worm.

At this the monsters bared their giant, broad-edged teeth, jutting from their bloody jaws, and greenish darts of poison spurted from their slimy eyes.

I, however, felt that now they judged me weak enough to conquer and become their prey; and already they were looking forward to their triumph.

But in the face of imminent destruction there rose in me the strength of desperation and I stood up to their assault.

I grabbed the first and closest of the demons —his body seemed a chilly, viscous mass— and grimly throttled him, though nearly overcome with loathing, until exhausted he collapsed.

At that instant the entire horde surrounding me fell back in shock, like paralyzed, so that by having vanquished one of them I at the same time had defeated all.

Fearfully crouching on the ground they now were anxious to escape my eyes.

The more closely I moved toward them, the farther away from me they quickly fled.

And as the moon began to pale and in the eastern sky the new day cast its light, all these repulsive creatures clung fervidly together, slowly rose above the earth and drifted away like a dark, far-stretching bank of clouds.

But I could feel their death was near and that they could no more escape their end.

The sun then having risen red as blood above the fiery sea, its blinding radiance dissolved the somber cloud, whose shreds of gold now faded in a world of light.

And suddenly the Master stood before me, offered me his hand and, looking joyfully into my eyes, said this to me,

"I am glad to greet you again in the light of day. I suffered much concern on your account, but now the twilight realm has known you as its master. You henceforth are able to enter that realm without danger whenever you wish and all its demons shall be lying at your feet."

CHAPTER ELEVEN

INDIVIDUALITY AND PERSON

THERE HAD BEEN SOME DISCUSSION about the various forms that human beings take to be expressions of their *timeless self.*

Finally, one asked the Master to clarify the question, and he said,

"What he that seeks eternal life must do—both here and in all states of posthumous existence—is not to disavow his *individuality* but, in his inner being, to reject, to disregard the *person*, which both the outer world and his own unawareness force upon him like a mask.

"No longer stirred by wishes as a *person*, his inner life may nonetheless be moved by wishes aiming at more distant goals—beyond his personal state—to loftier and purer heights, although such wishes shall have no effect unless they can engage the power of his will according to their purpose.

"Only wishes of that kind are truly rooted in the depth of *individuality*.

"What the *person* wishes, on the other hand, is always for those things to last which ought to pass away, and to accept as truth what is but temporal illusion.

"The fulfillment of such wishes never leads to higher ground but only hinders one's unfettered free ascent.

"Wherever properties of *person* are still pampered and indulged, in wishes or in thought, that which is eternal, uniquely *individual* has not yet found expression.

"Whoever would perpetuate his temporal existence as a *person* must be willing to see other things destroyed.

"For he continuously comes upon things other than himself that will be standing in his way.

"Also *individuality* seeks nothing but itself, but only to the end that in itself it may sustain all other things in being.

INDIVIDUALITY AND PERSON

"*Individuality* knows all existence unified within its very self.

"It cannot love itself without embracing, at the same time, all things else in being.

"It will not ever hate what constitutes the *person*.

"After all, it knows that none of it is real.

"It treats the *person* merely as the role an actor plays.

"It may respect the role to the degree that it permits the player to express himself as an eternal *individuality*.

"*I<small>NDIVIDUALITY</small>* <small>SEEKS ONLY</small> values that will heighten and lead to purer forms to structure all of life.

"Whatever will not serve these goals it shall ignore as *non-existent*.

"Eternal *individuality* and everlasting *self* are *one* within each other.

"*Person* imposes confining limitation.

"*Individuality* is infinite alike in space and time.

"No *individuality* could ever hinder any other in unfolding its own self.

"Each one rules an infinite realm of its own.

"In oneness with all other *individualities*, by them pervaded and pervading them, it apprehends them all within itself alone.

"Forever streaming from the source of final Being, *individuality* builds but its own existence—as one of final Being's infinitely varied forms.

"Even so, it will experience all other, similar forms within itself, aware that, in respect to structure, it is itself identical with all.

"No force outside itself could ever prove an obstacle, and nothing can destroy it, once it rests securely on its own foundation."

CHAPTER TWELVE

THE REALM OF THE SOUL

Here I shall unfold to you the teachings on the soul as they were known throughout the ages by the Luminaries of eternal Light.

This conveys the wisdom of the few whose lives are guided by the light embodied in these teachings to this very day.

Western schools teach other things; and even in the East you will not often come across these insights, which rest on the objective knowledge of those who speak from personal experience.

Nonetheless, whoever teaches other matters will lead you into error.

Listen, then, and comprehend within your heart.

Eternal from the Origin, without beginning, without end, abides the human spirit.

Eternally it lives within its own light's radiant substance—its very essence being light—because it is a *spark* of that forever self-begetting *sun* that without ceasing pours its hosts of fiery sparks into the depth of endless space.

Do not assume that *sun* is "God," for God is something different.

To make you see that difference is not a simple task.

I need to use a term employed in chemistry to help your understanding and so I would explain it saying:

God is the most purified *distillate* of the Spirit, not "the Spirit" in itself in its forever self-begetting conflagration.

The human being's individuated spirit, however, is like a single spark of that continuously blazing sun; a spark wherein the Spirit's most sublime distillate—the human being's *living God*—is able to beget itself, in infinitely varied forms.

Pouring forth its sparks throughout the aeons, the Spirit's Sun of the Beginning eternally engenders its own self.

Endlessly revolving, this blazing Sun hurls multitudes of its scintillas into the Spirit's boundless space, as hierarchies abiding in the Spirit.

The primal sparks emitted by that Sun are still, to use this image, gigantic suns in their own way; but they in turn unceasingly pour forth additional sparks, additional suns, which equally continue to emit still smaller, weaker sparks as flaring suns.

The spiritual scintilla that has confined itself within the human creature—the spark of timeless Spirit through which alone the mortal human *animal* becomes a *human being*—is not by any means the smallest of these sparks.

The best way you may form a concept of the "size" of the eternal *human* sparks in their relationship to other, larger and smaller, sparks or suns within the Spirit is to consider the earth in comparison with other, larger or smaller, stellar bodies in the universe.

It was given in the nature of the spiritual scintilla which came to make itself a prison in the human animal body that it choose the realm of the soul as the dimension of its creativity; and finally, in order to gain domination also in the realm of matter, it strove to find a body of material substance.

Yet such a body it possessed already; a form that, while connected with material life, was independent of the laws that govern matter.

Only the fact that the spiritual scintilla, frightened by the physical effects inherent in its powers, bound itself to the body of the animal creature on earth finally caused its quest to bring about its "fall."

Yet while this quest led to its "fall," it likewise proved to be a searching of profoundest depths, in which a consciousness of new dimensions can be born.

Although the spiritual scintilla through its fall had lost the consciousness of being one of the eternal Spirit's suns, the inner force, which nonetheless remains its own, impels the fallen spirit to rise again to its own former being, to know itself once more upon its ultimate return, which then it will experience in a state of glory that is fully apprehend only from the depth to which it had descended.

From its primordial origin, each of these smaller spiritual scintillas, these solar sparks, is bound to strive toward the dimension of the soul; it merely is the vehemence of its pursuit that makes it overshoot the actual goal it sought to reach.

It is the realm of the soul toward which each spiritual scintilla needs to make its way in order to be able to structure its own world and manifest itself in its inherent powers.

Before it reached that realm it only knows its own self to exist, is conscious only of its own pure being.

In the realm of soul, however, it finally becomes aware of the effective powers it possesses.

Only in the realm of the soul can the scintilla of the Spirit seek its own divine potential;

and only in a spirit seeking *God* can the distillate of the Spirit ever gain its form—can, in other words, the *living God* be *born* within the spiritual scintilla.

IN THAT ETERNALLY revolving Sun of Spirit, which in its boundless magnitude is conscious only of itself; the Sun that pours its solar sparks unceasingly into the Spirit's depth of space, there is no need that *God* exist; for all of Being here is undivided radiant Oneness.

For *God* to be, however, there is need for something conscious to exist that is not *God*; does not revolve within itself alone, sufficient in itself and perfect.

Even as the daylight's whiteness can be split into a range colors, light and dark, so also must the Spirit's primal oneness separate itself into a spectrum, as it were, of rays if *God* is to be *born* within the Spirit.

Within the Spirit's light, whose whiteness shows no colors, hues of darkness must appear, in order that the Godhead's light of golden white may manifest its essence.

THE REALM OF THE SOUL

That event, however, is made possible in the realm of the soul.

Each human spiritual scintilla submerges itself in this realm, where then around it gather, much like crystals form within a supersaturated salt solution, the countless combinations of elements which in your Western teachings are regarded as the human being's "soul."

Here in the West you believe this "soul" is like a finite and distinctive body, composed of some invisible fluidic substance; and your teachings have the body of this "soul" come into being at a mortal's birth into an earthly organism, whose owner would from then on never be able to lose it. In other words, while having come into existence in the realm of time, that "soul" would henceforth live forever.

In truth, however, the human being's *soul* is not by any means that kind of self-contained and compact body, because the realm of the soul is an invisible ocean of fluid energies wherein no permanent, unchanging forms exist, other than the countless particles of energy one might describe as *atoms* of the soul. These *atoms* are the elements composing individual *souls*. In every case, however, their numbers exceed thousands upon thousands.

As soon as the eternal spiritual scintilla—your true *self* in the highest sense—approaches the realm of soul, as soon as it becomes immersed in this fluidic sea, billions of these energies will rapidly collect around it and become illuminated by the Spirit's individuated light.

The spiritual scintilla, however, strives to probe forever deeper levels, down to the bottom of that sea, where it confronts the fear-unleashing forces that mislead it to seek shelter in the outer realm of matter at its densest; so that it merges itself with the human animal creature, thereby losing knowledge of its timeless self.

Born then from a mother's body it becomes a human being here on earth.

Yet even at the bottom of that sea and in its garb of flesh and blood the spiritual scintilla remains enfolded by the ocean of the soul.

In time it learns to recognize the forms that crystallize around it and begins to see them through its own, if deeply clouded, inner light.

IT IS NOT THE FIRST time that these elements had crystallized such forms.

In fact, they had already been at work in countless spiritual scintillas in the past and shall continue to detach and reconnect themselves again and again, in similar forms, until the impulse that initially had forced them to take form has reached complete fulfillment, in that a human spiritual scintilla was able to unite all elements of such a form within its own inherent will.

FROM THIS RESULTS that in your *soul* you may hear sounds that were not for the first time only heard in you and in your present life; and that misled believers in the East to think it is the human being's *spiritual scintilla* that was fated many times to suffer incarnation in a mortal creature body.

Things are not, however, as people in the East believe and as at this time many even in the Western world appear inclined to think.

Although there may be cases when an incarnation ends in failure, as it were—as a result of which the human spiritual scintilla is driven to succumb a second time to its profoundest fall—these exceptions are so rare that they do not affect the rule.

Suicide, early death, as well as an excessive "incrustation" in the creature body's rigid shell may generate the impulse toward a second incarnation, but even here such cases are quite rare.

You think that you perhaps detect within yourself a trace of human beings who had lived in ancient times?

Once you have awakened in the Spirit you even can recall entire human lives; and such a recollection of your soul's inherent energies is then relived by you—the person living here on earth today—but you were not the one whose life you thus experience as your own.

You merely carry in yourself those forms of soul-borne energy that had come into being in that other person's life but which did not attain fulfillment of their drives.

THE REALM OF THE SOUL

What you have come to call your "soul" is a continuously changing complex within the ocean of the soul's dynamic elements—in the dimension of the soul.

Every action, every thought, and every impulse of your will can instantly cause changes in that complex.

Unless you are entirely encrusted in material things your "soul" will change from year to year; and, according to the teachings found in ancient wisdom, every seven years you surely will discover completely different dynamic forces active in your "soul."

Certain combinations of these energies will also in your soul repeat their striving toward fulfillment; and those you did not help to reach that goal while you are still alive you then bequeath to human spiritual scintillas that must in future ages live their lives on earth.

With that inheritance is always given the potential of remembering the earthly life of the mortal who left it.

It thus is also possible that someone else in future days has memories of your existence and then mistakenly become convinced of having lived *your* mortal life.

The ocean of the soul envelops you in such a way that you could never reach its limits, let alone transcend its shores.

By virtue of the forms that in your soul have crystallized at a particular moment—forms that are continuously changing—you shall always find yourself "in motion" in this fluidic "sea of the soul," which is invisible to mortal eyes.

But even following the death of the material creature body, nothing in that state shall help you gain unchallenged power till finally the last of all the impulses you had initiated in your days on earth has reached complete fulfillment in future human lives.

Yet after death you can no longer change the forms your soul shall have attained.

Such as they were the moment when your mortal body could no more sustain the stress of physical existence, you then will have to

THE REALM OF THE SOUL

keep them until the last remaining impulse you had once initiated has reached fulfillment in a future human life.

Even so, you need not be afraid.

Those who became unchallenged rulers in the realm of soul before your time will there be by your side; nor shall the time until your final "resurrection" go to waste, even if, in human terms, it were to be "millennia."

But just as *you* shall then be waiting for the last or your "redeemers," human spirits who in ancient days had lived on earth in flesh and blood are waiting now—for you.

See that what you bear within you of those earlier lives will reach complete fulfillment in your days!

Again, do not initiate new impulses unless you will yourself direct them toward complete exhaustion in your life on earth!

To be sure, you also should create new impulses, but only such you can with certainty resolve in your own day, according to the best of human judgment.

What do you gain by generating impulses that would, in your opinion, benefit all humankind, but if your hand then lost control of what you started, before you could yourself complete what you began?

You only would cause suffering, for others and yourself, since in the realm of the soul no action is effected without its consequences being felt through the millennia.

THE TEACHINGS ON THE soul, such as the Spirit's *Luminaries* have known them since the dawn of time, and likewise guarded by the very few that gained their knowledge through experience, I here have shared with you in simple terms.

If your eyes see clearly and are not blinded by mere prejudice, you will find echoes of these teachings in many doctrines interweaving insights based on truth with error-fraught illusions, in that way creating multi-colored arabesques.

Perhaps, however, I too heavily laid hands upon your favorite beliefs, the superstitions closest to your heart?

THE REALM OF THE SOUL

But do not let what you believe deceive you!

Neither in the world of physical perception, nor in the realm of the soul is anything that happens ever influenced by what you think.

Paths securely built on solid ground pervade all realms throughout the universe and on these paths alone will life and work proceed.

You cannot open novel roadways, even if, in your opinion, the ancient paths no longer serve their purpose.

There are many in the Western world today who feel there is a core of truth concealed within the teachings of the East.

However, they embrace with blind belief what they should sift with open eyes.

You will not find in any people's writings a doctrine that is "finished" and "complete" and might reveal the fullness of all truth.

But everywhere you search you will encounter traces of the truth, and if you recognize them you are blest.

You thus shall not waste time pursuing endless and misleading byways.

Our aim is also merely to protect you from such error-ridden paths.

Let these teachings serve you to that end!

We give you only what we know with certainty, drawing on our *self-experience*, after we, in bygone days, could likewise but "believe" when first we heard these teachings.

CHAPTER THIRTEEN

ON FINDING ONESELF

IN THE DAYS WHEN I STILL WENT through bitter struggles to pass the tests my Masters had to make me undergo before they could admit me to their circle, I once had been the guest of a distinguished Master of whom no one in his environment would ever have suspected that he was a Luminary of eternal Light.

On one of those delightful evenings of the South, when by ourselves we strolled along the shore of the sea, I asked him how it was that he himself had once attained enlightenment, given he was constantly burdened with affairs of the world; and the man before whom thousands trembled, being subject to his rule, began to answer me and said,

"Indeed, even on me, the unworthiest, the Spirit once had granted the last of its secrets; and since that day I did have power to be wise.

"Even so, I very seldom acted wisely at that early time; for far too deeply had the marrow of my bones become ingrained by that which sundry doctrines of the West and East had by their praises caused me to accept as 'wisdom.'

"It is not all that easy to erase the many things that have informed our flesh and blood, inherited from our forebears and later strengthened still by teachings both at home and school.

"But then there came a day when finally the Spirit spoke to me these words in fear-inspiring mightiness,

'All evil is but *fear*!'

'You still let fear suppress your faith in wisdom, and now you call that fear your *doubt*!

'I give myself to none who fears me!

'I give myself to those alone who, free of fear, can think and feel and act—within me!

'Doomed is who still seeks for me without!

'Doomed whose self is still divided, not born as yet and one with me!

'Everything external is set before you to be overcome!

'I, however, am the One who masters all that is without and everything within; and nowhere but in me—united with me as one self—shall you at any time gain domination over everything within you and without!'

"Had I always since that day been guided by the word of wisdom, I truly should have acted wisely.

"Yet in my bones and blood there also lived in me another voice, which said to me,

'You simpleton!

'How can you make yourself believe such words?

'Do you not know that you are merely earth? A mortal creature walking on two legs?

'How could you seek to unify yourself with Him who rules as lord and master over every outer world and every world within?'

"And often did I let this voice deceive me; indeed, at times I believed it even more than the word of wisdom.

"I grew small and wretched in my sight; for I trusted that other voice and thus succumbed to fear—fear of the highest of all powers, which sought to give itself to me.

"And so I once again fell back into a state of gloom and torment, forgetting what I had been granted in those hours when I already was united with the Spirit.

"But after having for a long time lost my path, I still came in the end to see the day when that which earlier I had received as *revelation* and as a special *gift* at last was to become a *permanent, continuous experience.*

"Only now was I myself made living light.

"I DO NOT KNOW WHAT I had been before, nor do I want to know it.

"Be it that I was a mere cadaver who dwelled in tombs as food for loathsome worms, or but a phantom likeness of myself—enough that now I was aware of who I am and never can forget it anymore.

"I THINK IT ONLY WAS a little grief of earthly life which to my mind appeared so great that it enshrouded all the world before my eyes.

"To this small grief, however, I am in debt for my recovery.

"When all the world to me seemed lost in gloomy misery I found at last *myself*—even though I long had been deluded thinking I had surely found 'myself' already.

"BUT WHILE I IN THE past had truly known myself at times, for moments or inspired hours, I later felt again divided, and the other one, who was a phantom or a corpse, would once more take possession of my being.

"Now at last I had the strength to strangle him to death; nor did I show him any mercy, however much he begged and whimpered when he realized that I no longer meant to suffer him within me.

"Thus at long last had I risen from the dead, within myself.

"Today I shudder looking back on what I once had been.

"Radiant now within my own eternal light, I henceforth *know*—not merely comprehend—the one *I* truly *am*.

"I, who thus became *myself,* can never again serve any other outside of *myself.*

"Only from that time on was I able to make others obey my commands; and now they do as they are told because they sense they are obeying one whose orders have authority.

"Before that day, however, I merely was compelled to issue orders; and I was then obeyed with only anger and resentment, because like many others who are forced to issue orders I did not have authority."

CHAPTER FOURTEEN

ON THE ELDER BROTHERS OF MANKIND

Y̲ou well may for some time have had the question on your mind how I myself had come to know those very few about whose work I have to tell you in my books.

You thus may want to know how first these sages came into my life, which happened long before I could have even dreamed of one day being made a member of their circle.

I fear you would dismiss the very first encounter as an instance of "hallucination" if it occurred in your life as it did in mine, in the early days of my childhood.

Perhaps you feel but little inclination to believe there is a way of "leaving" this body of flesh and blood without "dying," and that the few endowed with this capacity are able to journey, in their *fluidic* likeness, the greatest distances at almost the speed of thought; and also that in certain places and under strictly set conditions they are able, on occasion, to make their presence visible, tangible, and audible in such a way that you could not distinguish them from mortals of flesh and blood.

That faculty, however, is not by any means restricted solely to the authentic masters of the Spirit's Brotherhood, and many a legend may be rooted in the practice of this gift.

You cannot even be completely sure that you do not yourself possess that faculty; for many people practice it unknowingly, which is to say, that in their state of lucid wakefulness their mental consciousness is unaware of what they do while sleeping.

Here we find ourselves in a domain where our Western scientific disciplines do not yet know the border lines; a field they likely never will be able to explore more fully since all examination of this sphere requires the entire human being, not merely the mortal brain.

However, if a thing has not been "scientifically established," it does not, for most people, actually exist; and far be it from me to hold it against you if in this case you choose to side with the majority.

I cannot claim that my own way of thinking would be different had not my personal experience taught me otherwise.

Given that experience, however, I can tell you that such matters are not merely possible, but do occur more frequently by far than even those suspect who are "convinced."

THE FIRST ENCOUNTER with a messenger of the community to which I now belong occurred in the way I here described when I had barely learned my ABC's.

At first I took him for a beggar to whom my mother often gave some soup; but when he —and I hesitate to even speak of it—would come to me again and again, behind closed doors, or suddenly appeared before me in the open air, in field and forest, and just as quickly vanished, my childlike understanding sought another explanation, to which my fatherly friend and guardian kindly in his wisdom gave consent, even though it strictly speaking was not true.

Raised in the hands of a deeply religious mother, in a faith that worships "saints" before the "throne of God," I believed the messenger of the sublime community would surely have to be no other than a "saint"; and, furthermore, the very one for whom I felt especial veneration, and whose appearance I was fond of visualizing exactly in the way I saw my spiritual mentor on his "visits."

The traditional images depicting that "saint" could only confirm me in this faith; and when at last I found the courage to ask, I heard from the lips of that strange old friend these words, "Yes, my child, indeed; and later you shall know about me even more."

In childlike innocence I felt this to be unrestricted affirmation; even so I never said a word to anyone because the ancient friend had told me that as soon as I would speak about his visits he could no longer come to me; and I had grown so fond of him already that I could not imagine anything more terrible than losing him.

Perhaps this warning might not even have been necessary, given that the fear of mockery of every kind would have alone sufficed to seal my lips.

As time went by, I found the sudden coming and going of the old friend so very natural that I never even stopped to think how much these strange encounters differed from all other things in life.

When I had grown a few years older, however, his "visits" gradually became less frequent and in the end ceased altogether, which filled me with profound despair because I felt quite certain that my youthful "wicked deeds" must have deserved this punishment.

In matters of pedagogical discipline this proved quite salutary for a while, but when I found that all my efforts to become a really "good boy" had ultimately no effect I gave them up again and returned to my life in fields and woods like every other untamed youngster, so that I all but forgot the kindly old friend of earlier days.

Much later only did the feeling suddenly once more arise in me that in some way he still was very close; and that sensation always brought with it a sense of bliss one cannot easily describe.

Various experiences in my outer life would let me clearly feel what he considered good and what he wished me to avoid; but I never saw, nor heard, or touched him as I had in the past.

I would almost say it felt as if he were within me, or observed me from behind.

Years were to pass again until the day when I once more became acquainted with the sage old friend; this time under circumstances even a temperament more mystically inclined than mine would have considered strangely "mystifying."

On that occasion I met him in a very different way.

A visitor came to see me—a stranger at first glance, but recognized only too well a second later.

This time he did not appear in the oriental garments that earlier I had found so unusual, but dressed like a European, with the slightly casual elegance one sometimes finds in travelers from the East when they are wearing Western clothes.

I now was given duties which no longer made it possible to keep the meeting absolutely secret, at least from the beloved spouse who shared my life already in quite early years.

My life's companion was one among the first women who had successfully fought for the right to study at a university and was imbued with a thoroughly skeptical, materialist philosophy.

Letters that I had to send her at the time, because she was not present at that recent meeting, filled her with extreme concern because she feared that I perhaps had lost my mind. Only the cool-headed observation that my "madness" demonstrated too much "method" finally was able to dispel such dire thoughts, which, given her philosophy, were not all that far-fetched.

THE BOOK OF DIALOGUES

Later she would meet that visitor, and others of his kind, in person, in their bodies of flesh and blood, yet could not at that time foresee they one day would become her highly venerated friends.

Inspired by their explanations she gained clarity on much that earlier she had considered "legendary" in the writings of antiquity; and to the extent a woman may comply with occult laws, she did so that she might unearth the treasures hidden in the mysteries of ancient cultures; and what she found surpassed her expectations.

Early death prevented her from making public, in her own way, what she had discovered.

As for myself, however, I can only tell you that the mysteries revered in ancient times are to this day not yet extinct; merely the forms in which antiquity had known them have been lost.

I can vouch for the reality of an "initiation" whereof no manuscript or printed book will offer more than darkly veiled allusions.

ON THE ELDER BROTHERS OF MANKIND

I have knowledge of a Brotherhood—whose member I was obligated to become, as to that end I had been born—from which originated all associations here on earth that ever strove for highest wisdom in the Spirit.

Only very few belong to our circle.

What we are permitted to convey, we gladly offer to the world; what lies beyond, however, cosmic law forbids us to reveal.

In earlier centuries, many significant individuals were closely connected with our circle, even in the Western world—from the philosopher to the commander of armies, from the monk in his cell to the cardinal at the court of popes.

At the present age you rather need to look for those with whom we are in spiritual contact across the vast expanses of the East; and many are among them who are not pleased at all that the community of guides is now again —through me, and in transparent language —turning its attention also to the people of the West.

It was, however, necessary that this be undertaken; and it became my task because in

Western countries had begun to circulate more or less fantastic, fairy-tale-like rumors concerning the activities of such a "Brotherhood." Those tales were spread by gullible people, who might have thought to be in touch with us—having been misled in this belief by sundry curious holy men, which in the East are found in great abundance—after a woman in the West, who was a medium of phenomenal capacity, had learned that such a "Brotherhood" existed.

Throughout the world there also are found other groups that were not far from us at their beginnings.

Today we see their members pursuing ways that lead astray and into error.

We are not free to intercede.

We only are allowed to give to all what can to all be given.

We may do nothing more than show the way that leads to our sphere, whose influence is felt by spiritual senses.

You must not let the false belief delude you that the public appearance of a member of that Brotherhood could bring the world the benefits it can receive through us.

In outer life we find ourselves bound hand and foot by any number of unyielding laws.

We ourselves, in person, would have less to give than someone who had merely knowledge of and understood our teachings but was not bound by laws we must obey.

A violation of these laws, made all but unavoidable by personal involvement in the outer world, would sooner or later lead to quite preventable sacrifices; and not to risk the like wherever possible is our first and foremost aim.

About the path that leads into the sphere of spiritual influence of the eternal Brotherhood, that circle's nature and the cosmic context of its origins, I have sufficiently provided background in my books.

If you are willing to pursue that path you surely one day will be able to confirm the practical effectiveness of the dynamic spiritual energies, which are directed by that body as by a single integrated source.

These energies do not by any means proceed from us.

We merely are their mediators and appointed guides.

Beware, however, of merely toying with these energies!

Those who do not recognize the consequences of their actions on this path are playing a dangerous game!

Nor must you seek and treat what you may find through us as if it were a kind of earthly "science."

Again, you must not think that eating only plants, asceticism, abstinence from alcohol or sexual experience, nor any other strange eccentric way of life might either be required, or at least of benefit, if you are truly to achieve your goal.

All these ascetical and superstitious practices, supposed to realize a *spiritual* goal, are offshoots grown from one of the most sterile and pernicious attitudes toward life, which nonetheless paraded proudly in all cultures and every fashion of religious garb.

Those, by contrast, who would come to us that we may *spiritually* grant them what they seek should be above all else *clear-headed, quiet,* and *kind-hearted* human beings, but at the same time always *down to earth.*

Such seekers will be surely found by the sublime community of helpers.

Once they have been found, however, they will be able to receive that circle's gifts at any place on earth, in all conditions of their earthly life; and that the more effectively, the more they strive—beyond the aims they harbor in the Spirit—first and foremost to fulfill their earthly obligations toward themselves, their physical flesh and blood, and toward all mankind as a whole.

CHAPTER FIFTEEN

MYSTERIES OF MAGIC

T̲he glistening moonlight of̲ the South flowed in its palpable whiteness down the crevices of the barren mountains, filling the spacious valley with its olive groves like a shimmering lake.

The remnants of the marble columns of the long abandoned sanctuary shone like opals and a silken blanket of bluish white lay gleaming on the tiles of the floor, making all appear as if the site were covered with freshly fallen snow.

Two men walked silently across the sacred grounds of ancient times until they came to the foundation of a temple where they halted and sat down.

"This temple," said one of the two, "was founded by one of us, thousands of years ago, and for many a century our guidance inspired its priests.

"In the legends of the people it was later said that one of their gods had been the founder of this shrine.

"The site where now we find ourselves remains mysterious to this day, but its secret is no longer known by people of the present age.

"Wherever one of us in ancient times had founded such a temple he always chose a site where it was possible to generate an overflow of certain fluid energies within the earth, which cannot be by any means achieved at all locations on this planet.

"Today, the fountains of fluidic energies have long since ceased to flow at nearly all such places; even so, the forces that were able in this way to manifest themselves continue to be concentrated at such focal points; and so they follow still the selfsame paths that once had caused the founder of this sanctuary to build a temple at this site and also to prepare a priesthood to perform the sacred service.

"The priests who served these ancient sanctuaries were not at all from the beginning merely the practitioners of 'fraud,' as which they must appear today, when no one any longer even has an inkling of the mystery-enshrouded energies that were effective at such sites, by virtue of authentic *magic*; an energy whereof the present age knows nothing but its name, which has become synonymous with fraud and vaudeville sleight-of-hand.

"Even so, there truly was an art of *magic* in the highest sense; and there were also sites on earth imbued with magic energies; indeed, one still could find them even now if one knew how to search.

"Today, however, humans are no longer able to pursue this search; for in the course of time they let the senses wither in themselves which are essential for this purpose.

"The human being is connected with the planet's energies more closely than most people can believe, given they put too much trust in what their eyes can see.

"Countless powers of the earth would mortal man control if he were able to unfold the force within himself which all these powers must obey.

"If it were possible to teach how to unfold that inner power, all the world would soon be sitting at the feet of such a teacher.

"However, the unfolding of this power is connected with an inner growth; and before a person's inmost self has gained objective clarity and light, so that even with closed eyes he is able to see within himself whatever he wishes, he cannot find that inner power, nor ever learn to use it.

"He cannot even fathom what one speaks of if one were to tell him about the power that resides in him.

"Likewise, if one dares to mention the ability of "seeing with closed eyes" no one knows what is implied; and most believe they long have had that faculty, because they take the images of their imagination for the true ability of *inner seeing*.

"Nor can they ever comprehend the meaning if one says that everything within must first be clear and luminous; and they assume the light of reason and of logically constructed thought must be that needed clarity.

"They cannot grasp that high above such widely vaunted 'thought,' whose functions cease forever once the mortal body's elements disintegrate, there is another kind of thinking; one that causes thought itself to come alive and to grow conscious of its being; so that, detached from any thinking of the earth-bound mind, such thought in truth can *think itself*.

"THERE ARE PECULIAR 'teachers' in my homeland, and they have also found their way to you in Western lands, who drill their pupils to gain 'thought control'; and through that practice they believe one can achieve one's highest goal; because they came upon a faint reflection of the truth when they discovered that 'thoughts' are in some way connected with that quest.

"If in their folly they could grasp that no one ever reaches final truth in whom the *thought that is alive and conscious of itself* has not awakened and become unchallenged lord and master, they would be horrified to see how they subject themselves and others to a wholly useless torment, which has already driven many to the brink of madness, if not to the complete destruction of their minds.

"They have their pupils sit in silence and make them 'concentrate' upon a single thought, which they created in their brain.

"Their aim is to achieve a state that lets them and their pupils rest without a single thought for minutes at a time, or longer; and they believe that in this way they shall at last behold the light of truth.

"The only thing, however, they accomplish by this method is the ruination of their mortal body's nervous system and its brain.

"What they believe to be experiences of 'spiritual' life are never anything but the results of such unnatural stimulation of their bodies' nervous system."

"Given that," his companion interjected, "should one not rather warn against all 'concentration' of one's thoughts and every effort to 'control' one's mental life?"

The one who had spoken before, however, interrupted him and said,

"By no means, my friend!

"It all depends on the goal one seeks to achieve and how that advice is understood.

"If the intent is merely to control the kind of 'thinking' that is generated by the subtlest of physical organs and mediated through the brain—the very organs that allow it also to grow 'conscious'—and to prevent that 'thinking' from its aimless drifting, then you may at all times recommend the use of every means available in order to collect such 'thoughts' —which are no more than echoes of the *true* and *real* thought, reflected in the infinite kaleidoscopic mirrors of the brain—and so to gather them on one thing at a time.

"The thinking human mortal, who, objectively considered, is simply a more highly developed 'animal,' can only benefit in life on earth from the ability in this way to direct the workings of his mind.

"You also should instruct your readers that their mental thoughts must grow accustomed to obedience, lest they themselves become the servants of their thoughts.

"They need to learn to hold fast to such thoughts as may direct their actions and not to pay attention to the rest.

"They ought to bear in mind that they would merely cause their nervous system serious harm should they attempt to rid themselves of unproductive or pernicious thoughts by waging war against them, but that they shall defeat them without effort by consistently ignoring them, no matter how tenaciously such thoughts attempt to force themselves upon their consciousness.

"They need to recognize that they can never be completely without thoughts, except at the expense of their nerves, but that it lies within their power to cultivate the thoughts they want to harbor and, at the same time, calmly to let all unwanted thoughts pass by them, like images that have no longer any meaning.

"Such constant practice, which then in time turns into habit, imposes calm and order on the thinking process that depends upon the brain; and such a state of calm and order is the elementary condition if the human being one day is to reach the point at which the *living primal thought*, which consciously perceives itself, can finally be wakened from its sleep.

"Once a human being has awakened that primordial thought within—a goal, however, that hardly one among ten thousands ever reaches, because so few possess the courage to pursue it—that person then will see all 'thinking' in the only manner which, like other mortals, he had known before, merely as the shadow of a light he earlier had fathomed scarcely in its faintest rays."

"Everything you point out, venerated Master," his companion now replied, "Everything, indeed, I know as truth from personal experience, such as your great kindness led me to attain it.

"Even so, I would be grateful to you, apart from all the things that I myself have come to know, if I could hear from your own lips, while we are physically still close to one another, how you would in your own way represent, in human words, the power that lies hidden in the human being, conferred on us to be continuously passed along to others—the power that controls the secret forces of the earth."

And the venerable teacher answered,

"Do not think I lost the thread of what I wanted to convey.

"I merely sought to show you on these sacred grounds, and at this hour, the way your words should follow if you set out to tell the people of the Western world the truth about that timeless magic energy that you have come to know, but which they think is nothing more than a mirage of pious fraud and commonplace deception.

"And so I had to draw a clear distinction between what mortal humans understand as 'thinking' and the *living, self-aware, and conscious thought* which rules in us, given that we have awakened it, as the consummate 'Master' of all Masters; for truly it alone has granted us the power through which the hidden energies within the earth are made obedient to our will.

"You thus should tell the people of the West that their opinions of that power are mistaken. Tell them that not one among them ever could attain it on his own; for there is only One who holds the key to grant it in his hands; the One to whom we, too, give thanks for having gained it. Yet even we would not have come to own it, had not the *living, self-aware and conscious thought* awakened first within us from its sleep through many thousand years; had it not first in us ascended to immortal glory and dominion.

"People still believe this power is the function of some physical activity; that it demands of those who hold it the mastery of so-called 'magical' crafts; and that to be effective it requires the performance of mysterious 'rites' and 'ceremonies.'

"You should not seek to hide the fact that there indeed exists a kind of lower, merely temporary power over certain secret forces of the earth, which may be activated by such means; but you should also make it very clear that all these things have nothing whatsoever in common with the particular power over forces of the earth, and through them over cosmic energies, which one may speak of as the timeless magic of the Spirit.

"The practice of 'magic' that functions through external means, through 'rituals' and 'ceremonies', and thus requires the performance of certain physical actions, is related to the eternal magic of the Spirit in the same way as the thought that needs the earthly brain to manifest its presence is related to the *eternal, self-aware and conscious thought that thinks itself*.

"Try to make your Western readers clearly understand that the exclusive force at work within the sacred magic of the Spirit remains the *will* that is no longer ruled by any wish; and that such *will* is lord of vast domains of hidden forces of the earth—by virtue of itself.

Let them see with clarity that we ourselves had to accept the bonds of strict eternal laws when we attained that *will devoid of wishes*; and that we are by no means any longer 'free to do whatever suits our will'—a phrase that typically confuses 'wish' and 'will'—but that we had to unify ourselves with an eternal will, which now wills but itself in our will, without regard to our wishes—if they tended to oppose it.

"Tell the people who may heed your teachings that we have irreversibly subordinated all our wishes to a will that is eternal, so that our personal will is free of every wish, and now acts solely of its own accord, in service to the will that is eternal and forever unified with it as one.

"You surely will not be correctly understood at first, because the people in whose midst you are to live and offer guidance are far too much accustomed to forcing every new idea into the matrix of familiar concepts, until at last the new is rendered 'comprehensible' in terms of old traditions.

"Although you give them what in truth are mankind's very oldest teachings on the Spirit, you never must forget that fragments of these insights had reached them at all times, and that they used these elements to shape all sorts of doctrines, intermingling truth and error in bewildering arabesques.

"Again, I do not doubt that many of their newest teachers of supposed 'ancient wisdom' would gladly serve eternal truth, if only they were able to discern it, and had not been enthralled by the illusion that they already hold that truth within their hands.

"Your task will be to emphasize in clear and careful terms the difference between such 'teachers' and yourself; and as you know, we fail to share your confidence, which from a human point of view appears quite understandable, that those who were converted by their teachings might be best prepared and willing to receive the truth.

"If you decide to seek your pupils among believers who accept such error-laden doctrines, you do so at your own responsibility and risk.

"Even though you now are one with us as an integral member of a spiritual community, you nonetheless are free at any time to follow your own judgment; but you alone will then be held responsible for your decisions.

"If here you do not choose to follow our advice, that choice is wholly yours; and even when you later realize that we had counseled you correctly, this fact will prove a beneficial lesson, surely worth some disappointment.

"What we advise, instead, is this: Address your teachings to as many as your words can reach, as rain will fall alike on fertile fields and barren lands of rocks.

"Even among the rocks of deserted places, seeds are waiting that would come to life.

"It little should concern you whether or not you come to know of those who find the way to truth by following your teachings.

"Your given task is to uncover for the people of the West, in your own way, the wisdom of the *inner East*, which had so long been hidden under veils.

"You know that others of our kind, who always live in absolute seclusion, have the task of seeking out the sprouting seeds awakened by your teachings' beneficial rain, and who then strive toward their unfolding in the Western world.

"You never must let anyone, whoever it might be, persuade you to assign yourself a task that has not been conferred on you by us, the spiritual Brotherhood of the eternal hierarchy.

"Nor should you ever grow discouraged if you do not see any signs yourself that what you teach is having some 'success.'

"Your task is to make public, again and again, the insights you have come to know. You are consistently to offer, in like or similar words, the same authentic teachings, without regard to those who listen or seem inclined to heed your words.

"Our will—as an integral spiritual body—is that you, our Brother, make it possible for people in the West to recognize that even in this day and age the ancient 'mysteries' are still alive, of which the educated among them know from history.

"We want an age of new, profoundest spiritual awakening to dawn on earth; and we are confident the people of the West shall one day share with us the ripened harvest from the seeds we have presented them through you.

"You understand that, as a human mortal, you can only be the *mediator* of a wisdom you would never have attained, had not one of those who, since primordial ages, have been sending mankind help, consciously combined his will with your own spirit, long before on earth you would become your mortal mother's son.

"We know that you would have preferred to keep your knowledge to yourself and live your life in undisturbed obscurity. We must, however, obligate you publicly to offer teachings, even if we thereby charge you with a burden that at times may prove a heavy yoke.

"Tell the Western nations that the energies of magic on this planet have not ceased to function, but are merely waiting for a new humanity in order once again to manifest their powers.

"Teach all who seek to know how they may resurrect the magic pole that lies asleep within them.

"Teach them that their *readiness* to meet transcendent powers can bring these powers back to life.

"Teach them that all aspirations to experience higher forms of inner life depend exclusively upon their inner life's integrity, never on the forcefulness of their desires.

"Tell them that the message from the Spirit can only be received when perfect calm has settled on a soul.

"Tell them that the faculties their souls possess reveal themselves in only fleeting glimpses to their present consciousness.

"Teach them not to put their trust in anything except their own eternal, inmost *self*, which automatically attracts whatever help it needs.

"Tell them that all confidence must, in the end, be confidence in *life*, in one's own *self*, in truth must be *self-confidence*.

"Tell them this,

"The wellspring of all powers granted you resides in your eternal *self*.

"Within your *self* alone can you discover what you truly are.

"*Self* is the mirror reflecting all reality.

"The *self* remains the source of knowing ultimate reality and final truth.

"The *self* becomes the forum on which you shall encounter every spirit found in timeless life.

"Within the *self* resides the power that can learn to rule all energies in being.

"The *self* abides eternally in silence.

"Those who attain the state of timeless silence can find within the self the highest powers.

"Within the *self* you find the all-embracing Spirit of Eternity.

"Nowhere but within your *self* can your eternal living God be born.

"The body of this earth, however, must learn to trust and to believe in this eternal *self*.

"Also tell your readers this,

"No one reaches consciousness of his eternal *self* who is unable to forget what he had been before.

"The *self* is not some given 'thing,' some object one might grasp; nor is it any kind of 'being.' It is instead a 'no-thing'. Yet this No-thing is the all-embracing Everything—the form through which all things in being recognize themselves as One.

"Only in this 'Nothing' rests your true existence.

"Once you apprehend that 'Nothing' as your *self* you shall have found within you everything that is in being.

"Consciousness of *self* is being conscious of possessing in oneself the very center of all being.

"C‍ONVEY THESE TEACHINGS to the people in the Western world who put their trust in what you give them and you shall guide them to their highest goal.

"The *highest goal* of no two mortals is the same.

"Different in magnitude like the stars in the heavens are also the highest goals.

"Yet all who seek are able here on earth to reach—in their own given way—the highest goal that only they are destined to attain.

"Guide all who put their trust in you to *their* own highest goals; but warn them not to make those highest goals their own which very few can reach in any age.

"Tell them it suffices to have reached one's proper highest goal, but that it leads to ruin to pursue another's, even if it ranked immeasurably higher than one's own.

"In this manner guide the people of the West on straight paths to the light which at this time they still attempt to reach by devious ways, assuming it could not be found by other means.

"I now shall leave you in my mortal body's form and other members of our Brotherhood will meet and speak with you in words of earthly language.

"None of them, however, will have to give you different advice to guide you on your path; and in a little while you likewise shall advise yourself in this same way; for even as we are of *one* view in the Spirit, so, too, will each admitted to our circle soon find himself of one mind with us all in everything he must determine on his own."

WHILE SUCH INSTRUCTIONS were imparted, daylight slowly had begun to dawn and now the first rays of the rising sun already bathed the mountain peaks in golden light.

THE BOOK OF DIALOGUES

In the distance far below, the Aegean Sea lay silently in darkest blue.

Now people came along the road that led close by the ruins of the ancient sanctuary. They had with them an animal to carry burdens and were waiting for the venerable Master.

The latter now embraced his younger Brother, bidding him farewell, mounted the animal and joined those people as they traveled onwards, returning to his home in distant lands. The younger man, however, having accompanied the little group a short part of the way, after a last brief greeting finally turned back and, in the early rays of the morning sun, returned to his lodgings, weighing his venerated Brother's words in his heart, firmly resolved to act in their spirit.

CONCLUDING THEN THIS *Book of Dialogues*, I let you listen to a conversation, similar to many others, which were the cause that made me write the books I publish.

Many a year now lies between that night among the ruins of the ancient sanctuary and the pupil there instructed has long ago dispensed with asking questions.

He long since has become in all respects his Brothers' equal.

The task he was assigned, however, has only just begun to be fulfilled.

May the present *Book of Dialogues* also contribute to fulfill that task!

May it bring you clarity and answer many questions!

REMINDER

"Yet here I must point out again that if one would derive the fullest benefit from studying the books I wrote to show the way into the Spirit, one has to read them in the original; even if this should require learning German.

"Translations can at best provide assistance in helping readers gradually perceive, even through the spirit of a different language, what I convey with the resources of my mother tongue."

From "Answers to Everyone" (1933), *Gleanings*. Bern: Kobersche Verlagsbuchhandlung, 1990

Other Works by Bô Yin Râ published in English translation:

Bô Yin Râ:
An Introduction to His Works

Contents: Preface. About My Books. Concerning My Name. In My Own Behalf. Essential Distinction. Résumé. Comments on the Cycle <Hortus Conclusus> and the Related Works. Brief Biography of Bô Yin Râ. The Works of Bô Yin Râ.

The Kober Press, 2004, 117 pages, paperback. ISBN 0-915034-10-7

This book presents a summary of the essential features that set the author's works on final things apart from the innumerable publications, old and new, that seek to answer questions which thinking minds have asked in every generation. Traditionally, such answers draw upon beliefs, accepted faith, and speculative thought, culminating in systems of religion and philosophy. Rarely have solutions rested on objective insights into the dynamic structure of reality, embracing both its physical and spiritual dimensions. But in addition to providing such direct descriptions of these aspects of reality, the author's books are helpful guides that let the readers gradually develop their inherent faculties so that they may experience this reality themselves. For readers having sensed the nature of this ultimate experience the concepts "spirit," "soul, "eternal life," and "God" are then no longer merely abstract notions based on hope and faith, but have become realities that form the human being's timeless essence, even as they underlie all aspects of creation.

In the first chapter of this *Introduction* the author discusses the origin and purpose of his books; how they should be used; for whom they are intended, and what their application may accomplish. Here he also stresses that his writings neither are opposed to, nor written to support, any particular religious creed, even though the followers of all persuasions may benefit from what they have to offer to all who seek to know.

The following chapter sheds light on the author's name and explains why his books are published under this spiritual proper name, which is not an arbitrary pseudonym, invented for the purpose of effective self-illumination, but expresses, in phonetic equivalents, the essence of his nature.

In the final chapter he corrects a number of misunderstandings of his books and person, typically prompted by hasty judgments, hearsay, or prejudice. Here he also touches on the common source of all authentic spiritual disclosures and stresses that objective insights into that dimension ought to be distinguished from the subjective mystical visions found in the different forms of religion.

The Book on the Royal Art

Contents: PART ONE: The Light from Himavat and the Words of the Masters. 1. The Luminary's Self-Disclosure to the Seeking Soul. 2. The Harvest. 3. The One whose Being is Infinity. 4. Know Thyself. 5. On the Masters of the Spirit's World. 6. Pitfalls of Vanity. PART TWO: From the Lands of the Luminaries. 1. The Threshold. 2. The King's Question. 3. The Pillar in the Mountains. 4. The Night of Easter. 5 Communion. PART THREE: The Will to Joy. 1. To All who Strive Toward Timeless Light. 2. The Teachings on Joy. Epilogue.

The Kober Press, 2006. 198 pages, paperback. ISBN 0-915034-13-1

This work is the first volume of *The Gated Garden*, a cycle of thirty-two books in which the author shows the way that lets his readers find objective spiritual truth within the light that darkness cannot conquer. In this opening volume the author discloses his own spiritual origin and sources and explains the reason leading to the publication of these books in our time. As the Western mediator of the oldest roots of ancient Eastern wisdom he also gives his readers the criteria to distinguish spurious echoes of that wisdom.

Of particular significance for Western readers is the chapter "The Night of Easter," which recalls the actual events preceding what would later be accepted as the Resurrection. In this context the book also touches on the Eastern wellspring in the teachings of the historical Master of Nazareth.

The concept "Royal Art" in the book's title refers to the Indian Raja Yoga, but here the term is used to denote a spiritual craft that far transcends the practices that are today suggested by that name.

As the portal to *The Gated Garden* this book is of particular importance in that is sets the tone and outlines the perspective from which all other volumes in the cycle should be viewed and understood.

The Book on the Living God

Contents: Word of Guidance. "The Tabernacle of God is with Men." The "Mahatmas" of Theosophy. Meta-Physical Experiences. The Inner Journey. The En-Sof. On Seeking God. On Leading an Active Life. On "Holy Men" and "Sinners." The Hidden Side of Nature. The Secret Temple. Karma. War and Peace. The Unity among Religions. The Will to Find Eternal Light. Mankind's Higher Faculties of Knowing. On Death. On the Spirit's Radiant Substance. The Path toward Perfection. On Everlasting Life. The Spirit's Light Dwells in the East. Faith, Talismans, and Images of God. The Inner Force in Words. A Call from Himavat. Giving Thanks. Epilogue.

The Kober Press, 1991. 333 pages, paperback. ISBN 0-915034-03-4

This work is the central volume of the author's *The Gated Garden*, a cycle of thirty-two books that let the reader gain a clear conception of the structure, laws, and nature of eternal life, and its reflections here on earth. The present work sheds light on the profound distinction between the various ideas and images of "God" that human faith has molded through the ages —as objects for external worship—and the eternal *spiritual reality*, which human souls are able to experience, even in this present life. How readers may attain this highest of all earthly goals; what they must do, and what avoid; and how their mortal life can be transformed into an integrated part of their eternal being, are topics fully treated in these pages.

What sets this author's works on spiritual life apart from other writings on the subject is their objective clarity, which rests upon direct perception of eternal life and its effects on human life on earth. Such perception is only possible, as he points out, if the observer's *spiritual* senses are as thoroughly developed to perceive realities of timeless life, as earthly senses need to be in order to experience *physical* existence. Given that authentic insights gathered in this way have always been extremely rare, they rank among the most important writings of their time, conveying knowledge of enduring worth that otherwise would not become accessible.

The Book on Life Beyond

Contents: Introduction. The Art of Dying. The Temple of Eternity and the World of Spirit. The Only Absolute Reality. What Should One Do?

The Kober Press, 2002. 161 pages, paperback. ISBN 0-915034-11-5.

This book explains why life "beyond" is not so much a different and wholly other life, but rather the continuation of the self-same life we live on earth. The difference between the two dimensions lies chiefly in the organs of perception through which the same reality of life is individually experienced. On earth we know that life through our mortal senses, in life beyond it is perceived through spiritual faculties, which typically awaken after death. At that transition, the human consciousness, which usually is unprepared for the event, is at a loss and finds itself confused by the beliefs and concepts of its former mortal life. As a result, the new arrival faces certain dangers; for, owing to these mental prejudices, the person is unable to distinguish between perceptions of objective truth and the alluring phantom "heavens" generated by misguided faith on earth.

To help perceptive readers form correct and realistic expectations, that they may one day reach the other shore with confidence and without fear, this book provides trustworthy guidance into spiritual life, its all-pervading structure, laws, and inner nature. Given the unbreakable connection between our actions here on earth and their effects on life beyond, the book advises how this present life may best prepare the reader for the life that is to come.

The Book on Human Nature

Contents: Introduction. The Mystery Enshrouding Male and Female. The Path of the Female. The Path of the Male. Marriage. Children. The Human Being of the Age to Come. Epilogue. A Final Word.

The Kober Press, 2000, 168 pages, paperback, ISBN 0-915034-07-7

Together with *The Book on the Living God* and *The Book on Life Beyond*, *The Book on Human Nature* forms a trilogy containing guidelines toward a new and more objective understanding of both physical and spiritual realities, and of the human being's origin and place within these two dimensions of creation.

The Book on Human Nature at the outset shows the need to draw a clear distinction between the timeless spiritual component present in each mortal human, and the material creature body in which the spiritual essence is embodied during mortal life. The former, indestructible and timeless, owing to its being born of spiritual substance, represents the truly human element in what is known as mortal man. The latter, physical, contingent, and subject to decay and death, is no more than the temporary instrument the spiritual being uses to express itself in physical existence. Given that the spiritual and animal components within human nature manifest inherently discordant aspects of reality, they typically contend for domination of the total individual. Experience shows that in this conflict the animal component with its ruthless drives and instincts clearly proves the stronger.

To help the reader gain a realistic understanding of the human being's spiritual and physical beginnings, by way of concepts more in keeping with humanity's advances in every discipline of natural science, the book explains, to the extent that metaphysical events can be conveyed through language, the timeless origin and source of every human's spiritual descent. It likewise shows that the material organism, now considered mankind's primal ancestor, existed long before it was to serve the spiritual individuation as its earthly tool. In this context the author points out that the traditional creation story, such as it has survived, is not simply an archaic myth, invented at a time that lacked the benefits of modern knowledge, but instead preserves, in lucid images and symbols, a truthful view of actual events. Events, however, that did not happen merely once, at the beginning of creation, but are a process that continues even now, and will recur until this planet can no longer nurture human life.

Even so, the principal intention of the present work, as well as of the author's other expositions of reality, is not so much to offer readers a new, reliable cosmology, but rather to encourage them to rediscover and awaken the spiritual nature in themselves, and thus to live their present and their future life as fully conscious, truly human beings.

The Book on Happiness

Contents: Prelude. Creating Happiness as Moral Duty. "I" and "You". Love. Wealth and Poverty. Money. Optimism. Conclusion.

The Kober Press, 1994. 127 pages, paperback. ISBN 0-915034-04-2.

Sages and philosophers in every age and culture have speculated on the nature, roots, and attributes of happiness, and many theories have sought to analyze this enigmatic subject. In modern times, psychology has joined the search for concrete answers with its own investigations, which frequently arrive at findings that support established views. Still, the real essence of true happiness remains an unsolved riddle.

In contrast to traditional approaches, associating happiness with physical events, the present book points to the spiritual source from which all human happiness derives, both in life on earth and in the life to come. Without awareness of this nonmaterial fundament, one's understanding of true happiness is bound to be deficient.

The author shows that real happiness is neither owing to blind chance, nor a capricious gift of luck, but rather the creation of determined human will. It is an inner state that must be fostered day by day; for real happiness, as it is here defined, is "the contentment that creative human will enjoys in its creation." How that state may be created and sustained, in every aspect of this life, the reader can discover in this book.

The Book on Love

Contents: Introduction. The Greatest of Compassion's Mediators. On Love's Primordial Fire. Light of Liberation. On Love's Creative Power.

The Kober Press,. 2005. 148 pages, paperback. ISBN 978-0-915034-12-3

Love, properly understood, is not merely, as the author explains, a human sentiment of varying degrees of intensity, inspired by particular objects and, like all feelings, subject to continuous change. Love is, instead, the highest of creation's elemental powers, giving life to and sustaining all dimensions of reality. The human sentiment called "love" is but a faint reflection of that cosmic force and ought to be distinguished clearly from its distant source.

Earthly love in all its forms is typically aroused by the desire of possession for an object. Celestial love, by contrast, is a spiritual energy that manifests itself beyond and free of all desire, independent of external objects. Human beings can partake of the celestial form of love, which then transforms their temporal existence by virtue of their timeless life, and thus will make them more than simply "sounding brass and tinkling cymbals."

In its initial chapter the book sheds light on the historical facts surrounding the life and teachings of the unprecedented figure of Jesus of Nazareth, who, more perfectly than anyone before or since, embodied love's celestial force in word and deed. Empowered by that highest form of love he found the strength to change this planet's spiritual aura in his final hour and freed all human beings of good will from ancient bondage.

The Book on Solace

Contents: On Grief and Finding Solace. Lessons One Can Learn from Grief. On Follies to Avoid. On the Comforting Virtue of Work. On Solace in Bereavement.

The Kober Press, 1996. 126 pages, paperback. ISBN 0-915034-05-0.

In this book the author shows how sorrow, pain, and grief, although inevitable burdens of this present life, can and ought to be confronted and confined within the narrow borders of necessity. Considered from the spiritual perspective, all suffering experienced on this earth is the inexorable consequence of mankind's having willfully abandoned its given state of harmony within the Spirit, a deed that also ruined the perfection of material nature. Although the sum of grief thus brought upon this planet is immense, human beings needlessly expand and heighten its ferocity by foolishly regarding grief as something noble and refined, if not, indeed, a token of God's "grace."

Understanding pain objectively, as a defect confined to physical existence, which, even in exceptional cases, is but an interlude in every mortal's timeless life, allows the reader to perceive its burdens in a clearer light, and thus more patiently to bear it with resolve.

While suffering, through human fault, remains the tragic fate of physical creation, the highest source of solace, which helps the human soul endure its pain and sorrow, continually sends its comfort from the Spirit's world to all who seek it in themselves. How readers may discover and draw solace from that inner source the present book will show them.

The Wisdom of St. John

Contents: Introduction. The Master's Image. The Luminary's Mortal Life. The Aftermath. The Missive. The Authentic Doctrine. The Paraclete. Conclusion.

The Kober Press, 1975. 92 pages, clothbound. ISBN 0-915034-01-8.

This exposition of the Fourth Gospel is not a scholarly analysis discussing the perplexing riddles of this ancient text. It is, instead, a nondogmatic reconstruction of the actual events recorded in that work, whose author wanted to present the truth about the Master's life and teachings; for the image propagated by the missionaries of the new religion often was in conflict with the facts. The present book restores the context of essential portions of the unknown author's secret missive, which the first redactors had corrupted, so that its contents would support the other gospels.

Written by a follower of John, the "beloved disciple," its purpose was to disavow the "miracles" the other records had ascribed to the admired teacher. His record also is unique in that it has preserved the substance of some letters by the Master's hand, addressed to that favorite pupil. Those writings are reflected in the great discourses which set this gospel text apart and lend it its distinctive tone.

Given the historic impact of the man presented in this work, an accurate conception of his life and message will not only benefit believers of the faith established in his name, but also may explain to others what his death in fact accomplished for mankind.

The Meaning of this Life

Contents: A Call to the Lost. The Iniquity of the Fathers. The Highest Goal. The "Evil" Individual. Summons from the World of Light. The Benefits of Silence. Truth and Verities. Conclusion.

The Kober Press, 1998, 126 pages, paperback. ISBN 0-915034-06-9.

This book addresses the most common questions people tend to ask at times when circumstances in their daily lives awaken their awareness of the many unsolved riddles that surround the human being here on earth. To be sure, philosophy and teachings of religion have offered answers to such questions through the ages, but as these often draw on speculation, or require blind belief, they can no longer truly satisfy the searching mind of our time.

It is against this background that the present book will guide its readers to a firmer ground of understanding, resting on objective insights and experience. From this solid vantage, readers may survey their own existence and its purpose with assurance.

As this book explains, the key to comprehending the meaning of this present life is, first, the insight that this life is but the consequence of causes in the Spirit's world and, thus, has of itself no meaning other than that fact. And, secondly, the recognition that material life is ultimately meaningless if human beings fail to give it meaning: by virtue of pursuing goals whose blessings shall endure. The nature of the highest goal that mortals can pursue provides the substance also of the present book.

Spirit and Form

Contents: The Question. Outer World and Inner Life. At Home and at Work. Forming One's Joy. Forming One's Grief. The Art of Living Mortal Life.

The Kober Press, 2000. 108 pages, paperback. ISBN 0-915034-07-7

The underlying lesson of this book is that all life in the domain of spiritual reality, from the highest to the lowest spheres, reveals itself as lucid order, form, and structure. Spirit, the all-sustaining radiant *substance* of creation, is in itself the final source and pattern of all perfect form throughout its infinite dimensions. Nothing, therefore, can exist within, or find admittance to, the Spirit's inner worlds that is devoid of the perfection, harmony, and structure necessarily prevailing in these spheres.

Given that this present life is meant to serve the human being as an effective preparation for regaining the experience of spiritual reality, this life must needs be lived in ways that are consistent with the principles that govern spiritual reality; in other words, ought to be lived according to the structure, laws, and inner forms of that reality. To show the reader how this present life receives enduring form, which then is able to survive this mortal state, the book sheds light on crucial aspects of this physical existence and advises how these may be formed to serve one's spiritual pursuits.

Worlds of Spirit
A Sequence of Cosmic Perspectives

Contents: Preface. The Ascent. The Return. Reviews of Creation. Epilogue.

Illustrations: *Emanation. In Principio erat Verbum. Lux in Tenebris. Te Deum Laudamus. Space and Time. Primal Generation. Seeds of Future Worlds. Emerging Worlds. Birth of the External Cosmos. Labyrinth. Desire for External Form. Astral Luminescence. Sodom. Inferno. De Profundis. Revelation. Illumination. Fulfillment. Victory. Himavat.*

The Kober Press, 2002. 96 pages, 20 full-color illustrations, hardcover. ISBN 0-915034-09-3.

If all the books of Bô Yin Râ, objectively considered, are unparalleled in the extensive literature on subjects touching final things—in that their author did not publish speculations based on faith or thought, but gave the reader fact-based insights into spiritual reality—the volume *Worlds of Spirit* occupies a special place even among these thirty-two unprecedented works; for in this book he integrated twenty reproductions of his paintings, representing *spiritual perspectives*, to illustrate selected aspects of his text.

While the works of the *Hortus Conclusus* cycle constitute the first authentic, comprehensive exposition of metaphysical realities, the paintings in this volume represent, in turn, the first objective visual renditions of spiritual dimensions in their dynamic figurations, colors, and inherent structure. Together with the written word—the book describes events experienced and perceived by an awakened human spirit—the images are meant to offer readers lucid concepts of nonphysical existence, and thereby to assist them in developing their own perceptive faculties.

www.ingramcontent.com/pod-product-compliance
Lightning Source LLC
Chambersburg PA
CBHW062220080426
42734CB00010B/1961